Terror, INC.

AL-QAEDA

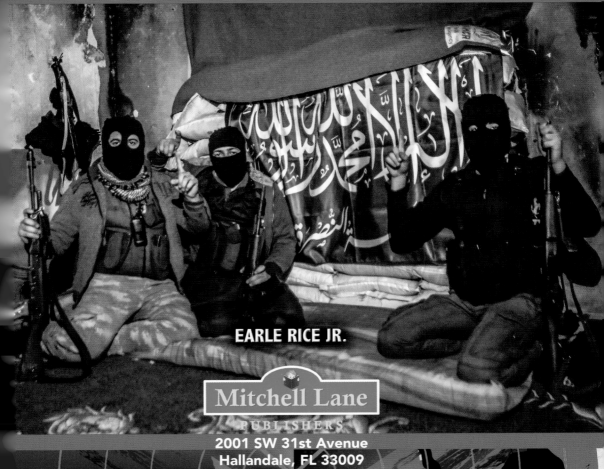

EARLE RICE JR.

Mitchell Lane
PUBLISHERS

2001 SW 31st Avenue
Hallandale, FL 33009
www.mitchelllane.com

Mitchell Lane
PUBLISHERS

Printing   1   2   3   4   5   6   7   8

Al-Qaeda
Boko Haram
Hamas

Hezbollah
Islamic State
Muslim Brotherhood

ABOUT THE COVER: Black-masked al-Qaeda militants in Aleppo, Syria, sit before a jihadist flag and indicate they are "number one."

ABOUT THE AUTHOR: Earle Rice Jr. is a former senior design engineer and technical writer in the aerospace, electronic-defense, and nuclear industries. He has devoted full time to his writing since 1993, specializing in military and counterinsurgency subjects. Earle is the author of more than 80 published books. He is listed in *Who's Who in America* and is a member of the Society of Children's Book Writers and Illustrators, the League of World War I Aviation Historians, the Air Force Association, and the Disabled American Veterans.

Library of Congress Cataloging-in-Publication Data
Names: Rice, Earle, author.
Title: Al-Qaeda / by Earle Rice Jr.
Description: Hallandale, FL : Mitchell Lane Publishers, [2018] | Series: Terror INC |
    Audience: Age: 9-13. | Includes bibliographical references and index.
Identifiers: LCCN 2017009126 | ISBN 9781680200478 (library bound)
Subjects: LCSH: Qaida (Organization)—Juvenile literature. | Terrorism—Juvenile
    literature. | Terrorism—Religious aspects—Islam—Juvenile literature.
Classification: LCC HV6431 .R523 2017 | DDC 363.325—dc23
LC record available at https://lccn.loc.gov/2017009126

eBook ISBN: 978-1-68020-048-5

Contents

Words in **bold** throughout can be found in the Glossary.

Foreword

Terror has plagued the world since men in caves flailed away at each other with sticks and stones. As the world emerged from **primeval** times and entered the ancient age, humans clashed on a larger, more advanced scale called warfare. Slings, arrows, and spears wrought havoc in the Golden Age of Greece and stained the glory that was Rome. Ethnic and religious strife followed close behind. In medieval times, crusading Christians and faith-based Muslims carved a bloody path across the Middle East with sword, lance, and scimitar in the causes of God and Allah. Americans engaged in "total war" for the first time during the Civil War, a war pitting brother against brother and fathers against sons at a cost of 750,000 lives. The 20th century introduced global wars that claimed the lives of tens of millions of combatants and civilians.

Today, international terrorism has become a form of warfare. The U.S. Department of Defense defines terrorism as "the unlawful use of—or threatened use of—force or violence against individuals or property to **coerce** or intimidate governments or societies, often to achieve political, religious, or ideological objectives." In many parts of the world, terror is a way of life. Militant Muslim extremists seek to rid Muslim countries of what they view as the **profane** influence of the West and replace their governments with fundamentalist regimes based on their interpretation of the religion of **Islam**.

The American way of life changed forever when 19 Islamist terrorists flew fuel-laden aircraft—flying bombs—into the World Trade Center in New York City and the Pentagon in Washington, DC, on September 11, 2001. Today, radical Islamist groups continue to be America's main threat of terrorism.

It should be noted that only a small minority of Muslims believe in terror as a strategy. A recent Gallup poll indicated that just seven percent of the world's 1.6 billion Muslims support extremist views of terrorism. The purpose of this book is to alert and enlighten the reader about that seven percent, while affirming the essential righteousness of the other 93 percent of Islam's followers. Peace be upon the gentle of mind, spirit, and deed.

The attacks on September 11, 2001, conceived by Osama bin Laden and carried out by 19 al-Qaeda terrorists, were devastating to the United States. With no remorse, the terrorists willingly sacrificed their own lives for their sadistic beliefs. It is a day the United States will never forget.

The North Tower of the World Trade Center in New York City erupts in flame and smoke after being rammed by a terrorist-piloted Boeing 767-200ER airliner.

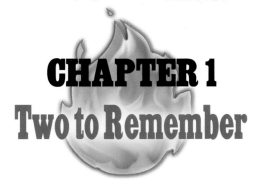

CHAPTER 1
Two to Remember

It was a morning made for poets who **wax lyrically** about rare and perfect days. The sky was bright blue and cloudless, and the air was crisp with a hint of autumn's nearness. New Yorkers hurried to work amid the early morning honk and hustle of a city that never sleeps. Towering high above Manhattan's concrete canyons, many office workers were already at their work stations. They could see forever in the sun-washed clarity of a bright new day. Or so it seemed. Rather, it was a day that would soon become etched forever into the **psyche** of every American.

Higher yet, from a vantage point in American Airlines Flight 11, attendant Madeline Amy Sweeney looked out at a much different world. At 8:44, Sweeney reported something wrong to a manager in the airline's operations center. En route from Boston to Los Angeles, the aircraft was flying erratically and descending rapidly. When the manager asked what she could see out of the window, she replied, "I see water. I see buildings. We are flying low. We are flying very, very low. We are flying way too low. Oh my God we are flying way too low. Oh my God!"[1] Those were the last words from Flight 11. It crashed into the North Tower of New York City's World Trade Center at precisely 8:46:40.

At about the same time, hijackers commandeered United Airlines Flight 175 from Boston to Los Angeles. Passenger Peter Hanson called his father in Connecticut to inform him of the hijacking. He said the hijackers had taken over the cockpit, stabbed a flight attendant, and possibly killed someone else in the front of the aircraft.

Several minutes later, Hanson called his father again: "It's getting bad, Dad. . . . The plane is making jerky movements. I don't think the pilot is flying the plane. I think we're going down. . . . Don't worry, Dad. If it happens, it'll be very fast. My God, my God."[2] Flight 175 slammed into the World Trade Center's South Tower at 9:03:11.

American Airlines Flight 77 had taken off from Washington, D.C. for Los Angeles at 8:20. About an hour later, passenger Nancy Olson called her husband Ted Olson, the **solicitor general** of the United States. She reported that the flight had been hijacked by men armed with knives and box cutters, who turned the airplane around. At 9:32, controllers at Dulles Terminal Radar Approach Control "observed a primary radar target tracking eastbound at a high rate of speed."[3] Five minutes later, Flight 77 smashed into the **Pentagon** at a speed of 530 miles an hour (mph).

United Airlines Flight 93 had departed Newark, New Jersey for San Francisco at 8:42. Forty-two minutes later, the pilot received a warning from United's flight dispatcher: "Beware any cockpit intrusion—Two a/c [aircraft] hit World Trade Center."[4] He asked the dispatcher to confirm the message. Before he received a reply, hijackers attacked the cockpit. Air traffic control in Cleveland received two messages from the plane, 35 seconds apart: First, "Mayday" amid sounds of a physical struggle. Then shouts of "Hey get out of here—get out of here—get out of here."[5]

At least 12 people on board phoned family, friends, colleagues, or others on the ground to share information about the attack. Five calls reported the intent of passengers and crew members to revolt against the hijackers and attempt to retake the plane. One passenger cut her call short: "Everyone's running up to first class. I've got to go. Bye."[6]

Another passenger, later identified as Todd Beamer, yelled, "Let's roll!"[7] The passenger assault began at 9:57. The cockpit voice

Firefighters work to douse the flames in the southwest E-ring of the Pentagon in Arlington, Virginia, on September 11, 2001, after terrorists flew a Boeing 757-200 into the building.

recorder captured the sounds of the ensuing struggle: thumps, crashes, shouts, and shattered glass and plates.

Another passenger shouted: "In the cockpit. If we don't we'll die!"[8] In an apparent attempt to ditch the attackers, the hijacker/pilot pitched the plane's nose up and down violently. Still another passenger yelled: "Roll it!"[9] The assault continued.

Another hijacker in the cockpit asked, "Is that it? I mean, shall we put it down?" to which the hijacker/pilot answered, "Yes, put it in it, and pull it down."[10] With perhaps only seconds before being overwhelmed by the passengers, he wrenched the control wheel hard to the right. The aircraft rolled on its back and headed down. Amid sounds of the continuing struggle, one of the hijackers started shouting "Allah is the greatest! Allah is the greatest!"[11] At 10:03:11, Flight 93 plunged into an empty field in Shanksville,

Pennsylvania, at 580 mph. Its intended target—either the White House or the Capitol, as determined later—lay about 20 minutes of flying time away.

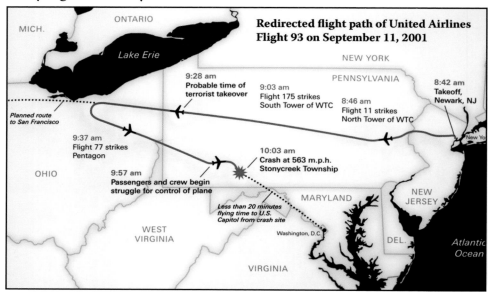

What had begun as a near-perfect day turned into one of the darkest and deadliest days in American history. It was September 11, 2001.

Ten years later, in a background report of the terrorist attacks, the National Consortium for the Study of Terrorism and Response to Terrorism (START) issued the following casualty report: "2997 people died as a direct result of al-Qa'ida's [al-Qaeda's] 9/11 attacks: 2764 deaths at the World Trade Center and on Flights UA175 and AA11, 189 deaths at the Pentagon and on Flight AA77, and 44 deaths in Shanksville, PA on Flight UA93."[12]

In a televised appearance a little over three years after the attacks, the Saudi Arabian leader of an Islamist terror group admitted for the first time that he had ordered the 9/11 attacks. He cautioned Americans that "there are still reasons to repeat what happened."[13] Two names few Americans had heard of before September 11, 2001, now resonated across the land: Osama bin Laden and al-Qaeda. Americans will never forget them.

Terrorism

The Planes of 9/11

Al-Qaeda terrorists hijacked four commercial airliners of two different types on September 11, 2001. American Airlines Flight 11 and United Airlines Flight 175 both flew a Boeing 767-200ER. The "ER" stands for "extended range." This aircraft could fly nonstop from New York City to Beijing, China. Flight 11 carried 81 passengers and 9,717 gallons of jet fuel. It crashed into the North Tower at 440 mph. Flight 175 slammed into the South Tower at 540 mph with 56 passengers and 9,118 gallons of fuel aboard.

American Airlines Boeing 767-200ER

American Airlines Flight 77 and United Airlines Flight 93 both flew a Boeing 757-200, four feet shorter and four feet slimmer than the 767-200ER. This aircraft was designed and marketed as a cost-saver. It features fuel efficiency and modified cockpits, which allows two pilots to do the work of three. Flight 77 carried 58 passengers and 7,500 gallons of jet fuel. It rammed the Pentagon at 530 mph. Flight 93 carried 37 passengers (including four hijackers) and slightly more than 7,000 gallons of fuel. It plunged into an empty field at Shanksville, Pennsylvania, at 580 mph.

In the hands of terrorists, four commercial airliners were turned into fiery flying bombs of mass destruction on 9/11.

United Airlines 757-200

Osama bin-Laden poses for this photograph in Afghanistan in 2001, cradling an automatic rifle. The al-Qaeda leader was seldom seen without a weapon in his possession or nearby.

CHAPTER 2
A Different Kind of War

Immediately after September 11, Osama bin Laden praised the terrorist attacks on the American homeland but denied responsibility for them. On September 20, President George W. Bush addressed Congress. With smoke still rising from the rubble of the toppled Twin Towers, he portrayed Osama bin Laden as a kind of terrorist godfather. He said "al-Qaeda is to terrorism what the Mafia is to crime."[1]

Eight days later, in an interview published in the Karachi *Ummat* (newspaper), bin Laden repeated his denial: "I have already said that I am not involved in the 11 September attacks in the United States. . . . I had no knowledge of these attacks, nor do I consider the killing of innocent woman, children and other humans as an appreciable act."[2] Evidence identifying two of the 19 hijackers as members of al-Qaeda suggested otherwise.

On October 4, British Prime Minister Tony Blair revealed Western intelligence information linking Osama bin Laden to Afghanistan's Taliban leadership. The Taliban was a militant Islamic group that had established a Muslim **fundamentalist** regime in Afghanistan. It had granted al-Qaeda safe haven there. The United States asked the Taliban to shut down all al-Qaeda bases in Afghanistan and turn over Osama bin Laden to American custody. The Taliban refused. On October 7, the United States began bombing Afghanistan and kicked off an air and land campaign called Operation Enduring Freedom. It toppled the Taliban regime about two months later. America's long "war on terror" had begun.

Al-Qaeda's connection to the Taliban grew out of the Soviet-Afghan War (1979-1989). The war, in turn, grew out of a volatile and unstable political environment in Afghanistan. In September 1978, a group of leftist military leaders staged a bloody coup in Afghanistan. The new regime established policies that included some features of communism and received financial and military aid from the Soviet Union.

Many Afghans believed these new policies conflicted with the teachings of Islam. They further resented Soviet influence on their government. Great numbers of Afghans rebelled. Soon, widespread fighting broke out between government forces and the rebels. The rebels called themselves *mujahideen* (holy warriors).

The Soviet Union grew concerned that the rebels might defeat the Soviet-friendly Afghan regime. At the end of 1979, the Soviets sent thousands of troops into Afghanistan to join the fight against the rebels. By the end of January 1980, the Soviet military presence in Afghanistan ballooned to some 80,000 troops. Their primary mission was to stabilize the Afghan government. Though the Soviets were better armed and equipped than the rebels, countries opposed to the Soviet Union's actions—especially the United States—sent arms and supplies to the mujahideen.

Volunteers from across the Muslim world poured into Afghanistan to fight with the mujahideen. Among the first was Osama bin Laden. He later noted, "In our religion, there is a special place in the hereafter for those who participate in *jihad* [holy war]. One day in Afghanistan was like one thousand days of praying in an ordinary mosque."[3]

At first, bin Laden's main contributions to the jihad came through his fundraising ability and his own open checkbook. He raised money, funded the construction of roads, tunnels, training camps, guest houses, and helped sustain the families of martyred fighters. When his former professor Abdullah Azzam established the Maktab al-Khidamat, or Office of Services, in Peshawar,

Soviet soldiers guarding a band of captured mujahideen—"holy warriors"—in Maiden Wardak Province, Afghanistan, in 1987.

Pakistan, bin Laden became its principal funder. Azzam used the Services Office as a clearinghouse for information about the Afghan War and a vehicle for channeling recruits into Afghanistan.

As the war continued, bin Laden felt compelled to take a more active role in the actual fighting. He was determined to seek **martyrdom** for himself. So he set up a base with several dozen Arab fighters next to a Soviet garrison at Jaji, near the Pakistani border.

In May 1987, during a several-week-long battle there, bin Laden earned his spurs in combat against Soviet troops, the Soviet-backed Afghan Army, and tribal militias. Egyptian film-maker Essam Deraz later described bin Laden in action: "I was near him in the battle, many months, and he was really brave. . . . [bin Laden] fought in this battle like a private."[4] Bin Laden established himself as a courageous fighter and a victorious military leader. Thereafter, his reputation attracted many followers to his cause.

In a later interview, bin Laden told CNN journalists Peter L. Bergen and Peter Arnett about the benefits he took from his jihad in Afghanistan: "What we benefitted from most was [that] the glory and myth of the superpower was destroyed not only in my mind, but also in [the minds] of all Muslims."[5]

In February 1989, the Soviets pulled out of Afghanistan. At some unrecorded point before then, bin Laden and about 40 of his mujahideen followers met at the al-Farouq camp in Afghanistan. Abu Ubaidah al-Banshiri, bin Laden's top military aide, addressed the group: "We [are] going to make a group . . . and there's going to be one [leader] for the group and it's going to focused on jihad, and we are going to use the group to do another thing out of Afghanistan."[6]

On August 11 and 20, 1988, bin Laden held two more formal meetings at his residence in Peshawar, Pakistan. Notable among the 14 attendees were Ayman al-Zawahiri and Jamal al-Fadl. Zawahiri, an Egyptian surgeon, was a member of the radical Islamic Jihad group. Al-Fadl was a Sudanese militant. Some sources recognize these meetings as the true birth of al-Qaeda, Arabic for "the Base." According to Egyptian journalist Faraj Ismail, it was Zawahiri "who got Osama to focus not only on the Afghan jihad, but regime change in the Arab world."[7] One war had ended; a new, global war was just beginning.

Osama bin Laden

Osama bin Mohammad bin Awad bin Laden entered this world on either March 10 or July 30, 1957 (sources vary). He was born in Riyadh, the capital of Saudi Arabia, to a Syrian mother and a Yemeni father. His father built a multibillion-dollar construction business in Saudi Arabia. He died in 1968, leaving an estimated $300 million of his fortune to Osama, the 17th of his 52 children.

Osama received a degree in civil engineering at King Abdul Aziz University in Jeddah in 1979. Shortly after graduation, he traveled to Afghanistan to join the jihad against the Soviet Union. He remained there intermittently for most of the next 10 years, using his wealth and engineering expertise to advance the Afghan resistance.

During the 1980s, Osama's strong **anti-Semitic** sentiments festered. He gradually began to hate the United States for its influence over Israeli policies. Years later, he recalled: "The event that affected me personally began in 1982 when America gave the Israelis the green light to invade Lebanon. . . . I cannot forget those unbearable scenes of blood and severed limbs. . . . They produced . . . a strong resolve to punish the oppressors."[8] In Osama's eyes, there was no greater oppressor than the United States.

Al-Qaeda chief Osama bin-Laden (center) holds a news conference in Afghanistan in 1998, bracketed by Ayman al-Zawahiri (left) and Mohammed Atef (right).

A convoy of Soviet personnel carriers winds through a crooked mountain pass during the Soviet withdrawal from Afghanistan in 1989.

CHAPTER 3
Building "the Base"

At al-Qaeda's inception, Osama bin Laden was named **emir** (leader) and Ayman al-Zawahiri Deputy Operations Chief, or second in command to bin Laden. Mohammad Atef, another founding member, was named military commander in charge of recruiting and training militants.

In an October 2001 interview with bin Laden, *Al-Jazeera* reporter Taysir Allouni questioned him about the scope of al-Qaeda's terrorist operations and his role in them. Bin Laden replied: "This has nothing to do with this poor servant of God, nor with the al-Qaeda organization. We are the children of an Islamic nation whose leader is Mohammad. . . . The name 'al-Qaeda' was established a long time ago by mere chance. The late [Abu Ubaidah al-Banshiri] established the training camps for our mujahedeen against Russia's terrorism. We used to call the training camps al-Qaeda [meaning "the base" in English]. And the name stayed."[1]

When the Soviets began their withdrawal from Afghanistan in 1988, bin Laden and Abdullah Azzam agreed that their group of volunteer mujahideen from Arab nations, known as Afghan Arabs, should not be allowed to disband. So they founded al-Qaeda. Al-Qaeda's initial goal was to carry the jihad beyond Afghanistan. The minutes of its founding meeting defined its goals vaguely as "to lift the word of God, to make His religion victorious."[2] Over the ensuing months and years, its aims and means of accomplishing them grew more detailed and refined.

Al-Qaeda operates under a general command structure. It is made up of the organization's senior leaders and their lieutenants, a Shura advisory council of the group's most trusted advisers, a supporting staff, and six committees:

Sharia/Political Committee—Issues *fatwas* (legal opinions by religious scholars).
Military Committee—Conceives and plans operations; manages training camps.
Finance Committee—Raises funds and conceals assets.
Foreign Purchases Committee—Acquires foreign arms and supplies.
Security Committee—Provides physical protection, intelligence, and counterintelligence.
Information Committee—Circulates propaganda.

Fighting between the mujahideen and the leftist Afghan government continued until 1992, when the rebels overthrew the government. But bin Laden's cause in Afghanistan ended with the Soviet withdrawal. He returned to Saudi Arabia in 1989 as a national hero and went to work for the family construction firm, the Saudi Binladen Group. The first thing he needed now was a new base of operations for his newly formed al-Qaeda and his Afghan Arabs. In 1990, bin Laden sent Jamal al-Fadl and Mamdouh Mahmoud Salim, another top al-Qaeda official, to Sudan to lay the groundwork for al-Qaeda's eventual relocation there.

On August 2 that year, Saddam Hussein's Iraqi Army invaded neighboring Kuwait and seemed also to be threatening Saudi Arabia. Bin Laden immediately approached the Saudi government with an offer to defend the kingdom. He planned to raise overnight an army of Afghan Arab mujahideen to pit against Saddam's forces, one of the largest armies in the world.

Turki al-Faisal, the Saudi intelligence chief, recalled bin Laden's attitude at the time of his offer. "He changed from a calm, peaceful and gentle man interested in helping Muslims," he said, "into a person who believed that he would be able to amass and command an army to liberate Kuwait. It revealed his arrogance."[3]

The Saudi royal family rejected bin Laden's offer. It actually ridiculed him and his proposition. It also warned him not to interfere. Shortly thereafter, 500,000 American troops, including many women, began arriving on Saudi soil in a buildup for the Persian Gulf War (1991). The presence of non-Muslims in the Land of the Two Holy Places—Mecca and Medina—incensed most of the Saudi *ulema* (religious scholars) as well as bin Laden. His hatred for Americans and the United States increased. "We believe that America has committed the greatest mistake in entering a peninsula which no religion from among the non-Muslim nations has entered for fourteen centuries,"[4] he declared. And he silently resolved to bring down the Saudi regime.

The Gulf War prompted bin Laden and al-Qaeda to reassess and dramatically expand their strategic goals. Abdel Bari Atwan, a controversial editor of pan-Arab publications, summarized these goals in five stages:

(1) Provoke the United States into invading Muslim lands;
(2) Enrage the *umma* (Islamic nation or community of believers) and incite a full-scale confrontation with American soldiers on Muslim soil;
(3) Expand the conflict throughout the region and engage the United States in a long war of **attrition**;
(4) Convert al-Qaeda into a set of guiding principles to transcend national boundaries and enable the establishment of franchises;
(5) Stretch the capacity of the United States to fight wars on many fronts and eventually cause its economic collapse.[5]

During and after the Gulf War, bin Laden began lobbying support for his anti-Saudi views from the ulema and Muslim activists. His activities soon led to more warnings from the Saudi government and eventually to his virtual house arrest. "The pressure that had been put on him turned to outright hostility," writes terror analyst Yossef Bodansky. "With Riyadh's belligerence

Afghan mujahideen undergo training to prepare for possible gas attacks during the Gulf War in their camp at Khafji, near the Saudi-Kuwaiti border. Arab allies joined the U.S.-led coalition to fight the Iraqi forces of Saddam Hussein. Volunteer mujahideen from Arab nations would later become known as Afghan Arabs and wage jihad—"holy war"—in Afghanistan and elsewhere.

mounting and fearing for the well-being of his extended family, Osama bin Laden and his family went into exile in the new haven of revivalist Islamism—Hassan al-Turabi's Sudan."[6]

Hassan al-Turabi was a Muslim scholar and Sudan's spiritual leader. He shared bin Laden's political agenda. He was also head of the National Islamic Front, which was dedicated to establishing a state based on *Sharia* (Islamic law). Omar al-Bashir was the **nominal** head of state, but al-Turabi wielded the real power behind the scenes. Bin Laden immediately endeared himself to both leaders. He supplied equipment to Sudan's military and pumped large sums of money into its struggling economy. Through his business investments and construction projects, he appeared to be a thriving entrepreneur. At the same time, he was covertly preparing al-Qaeda to go global with its operations.

Sharia Law

Sharia law is the law of Islam. Sharia literally means "the path" or "the road leading to water." It covers a wide variety of topics, including public and private behavior and private beliefs. It is derived from the actions and words of the Prophet Muhammad, called **Sunnah**, and the **Quran**, the sacred scripture of Islam.

In its most extreme form, Sharia is arguably the most strict and intrusive legal system in the world today—especially against women. Criticizing or denying Muhammad or the Quran is punishable by death, while thieves have their right hands amputated. Al-Qaeda's long-range goal is to spread this harsh version of Sharia law across the globe and establish a worldwide caliphate. A caliphate is an Islamic state ruled under Islamic law (Sharia) by a supreme religious and political leader known as a caliph.

Some scholars divide Muslim-majority countries into three categories regarding Sharia. Countries such as Iran and Saudi Arabia give Sharia official status. Others, such as Jordan and Malaysia, base their legal systems on a combination of Sharia (which covers family law), with **secular** courts covering everything else. Ethiopia and Kenya are examples of the third category, in which Sharia plays no role.

Protestors call for an end to democracy in the Maldives—islands in the Indian Ocean—in September 2014. They hoped to implement Sharia Law and replace democracy with a worldwide caliphate.

An aerial view of downtown Nairobi, Kenya, in the aftermath of an al-Qaeda car bomb attack directed against the U.S. Embassy (right) on August 7, 1998. The Cooperative Bank building can be seen at the left, with the Ufundi Cooperative House in the center. Thirteen days later, President Bill Clinton ordered cruise missile strikes on al-Qaeda, marking the first U.S. military action against the terrorist group.

CHAPTER 4
Going Global

By the summer of 1992, al-Qaeda was well established in Sudan. It boasted a roster of some 300 jihadists and many times that number of available contacts around the globe. Financing for al-Qaeda stemmed mostly from bin Laden's flourishing business enterprises. Additional funds came from supportive donors, mosques, sympathetic *imams*, and charities. As yet, however, al-Qaeda's mission remained vague. It lacked clearly defined targets, and it had yet to pull off a major act of terror.

The Gulf War had ended 18 months earlier, but the promised withdrawal of American troops from Saudi Arabia hadn't occurred. Their continued presence—at the request of the Saudi government—continued to rankle bin Laden. He wanted to strike out at the Americans, but that was easier said than done. He lacked the means to attack them in his homeland. So he pondered what to do. The answer came at year's end.

In December 1992, the United States began landing thousands of troops in nearby Somalia in a humanitarian operation backed by the United Nations. Their mission called for delivering food supplies to a starving Somali population caught in the middle of a bloody civil war. Bin Laden viewed the new American presence as yet another regional power grab by the United States. On December 28, al-Qaeda operatives set off a bomb at the Gold Mihor Hotel in Aden, Yemen, where U.S. troops lodged en route to Somalia. The attack, believed to be al-Qaeda's first, killed two civilians.

CHAPTER 4

The following February, Pakistani engineer Ramzi Yousef detonated a rental Ford Econoline van filled with high explosives in the basement of the North Tower of New York City's World Trade Center. The blast killed six people and injured more than a thousand others. Broadcast journalist John Miller viewed the destruction up close. "I had never seen anything like this," he wrote later. "It was total devastation. Of course, looking back, I now realize it was nothing."[1]

Yousef was not directly linked to al-Qaeda, but his collaborator, Sheik Omar Abdel Rahman—the so-called Blind Sheik—had financial ties to bin Laden. Six Muslim radicals were later convicted for the bombing, and bin Laden and 171 others were named as **unindicted co-conspirators**.

In early 1993, bin Laden sent a team of military advisors led by Mohammed Atef to Somalia to advise—and probably to arm— warlords fighting the weak central government. Defector Jamal al-Fadl later told U.S. officials of comments made by Abu Ubaidah al-Banshiri about the American presence in Somalia. According to al-Fadl, al-Banshiri said, "[W]e have to stop the head of the snake . . . the snake is America and we . . . have to cut off the head [of the snake] and stop them."[2]

On October 3 and 4, 1993, 18 American servicemen were killed while trying to capture two high-ranking Somalis. Somalis dragged the mutilated body of one of the dead men through the streets in the capital city of Mogadishu. Some 500–1,000 Somalis were killed in the fighting. Journalist Mark Bowden wrote the definitive account of the battle in his book, *Black Hawk Down*. A movie was later made. The U.S. pulled its forces out of Somalia several months later.

Bin Laden exulted over the American pullout. He told CNN: "Resistance started against the American invasion, because Muslims did not believe the U.S. allegations that they came to save the Somalis. With Allah's grace, Muslims in Somalia cooperated with some [Arab Afghans]. Together they killed large numbers of American occupation troops." He pointed to the American withdrawal as an example of the "weakness, frailty, and cowardice of the U.S. troops."[3]

Bin Laden soon fell into disfavor with both the Saudi and Sudanese governments over his activities. In 1994, the Saudi government stripped him of his citizenship and froze his remaining assets at home. Two years later, Sudan expelled him. By then, the Taliban had seized power in Afghanistan. Bin Laden saw it as a perfect place to relocate his operations. He moved there and developed close ties with Taliban leader Mullah Omar.

On August 23, 1996, bin Laden issued a fatwa against the United States, titled "Declaration of War Against the Americans Occupying the Land of the Two Holy Places [Saudi Arabia]." In it, he said there was "no more important duty than pushing the American enemy out of the holy land." He called on all Muslim brothers to concentrate on "destroying, fighting, and killing the enemy until by the Grace of Allah, it is completely defeated."[4] But bin Laden's war on America was not confined to Saudi Arabia.

In 1997, bin Laden ordered the militarization of al-Qaeda's East African cell. The following February, he issued a second fatwa against Americans: "The ruling to kill Americans and their allies—civilian and military—is an individual duty for every Muslim who can do it in any country in which it is possible to do it."[5]

Nearly six months later, simultaneous strikes by al-Qaeda at U.S. embassies in Kenya and Tanzania killed 223 people. In retaliation, U.S. President Bill Clinton launched cruise-missile strikes on al-Qaeda. The attacks marked the first U.S. military action against al-Qaeda.

Addressing the nation from the Oval Office, Clinton said, "Our target was terror. Our mission was clear: to strike at the network of radical groups affiliated with and funded by Osama bin Laden, perhaps the preeminent organizer and financier of international terrorism in the world today."[6]

On October 12, 2000, an al-Qaeda attack on the guided-missile destroyer USS *Cole*, while in port at Aden, Yemen, killed 17 American sailors and injured 39. Bin Laden's global war was just getting started.

The USNS *Catawba* (T-ATF 168), an ocean-going tug of the Military Sealift Command, tows the stricken USS *Cole* (DDG 67) into open sea from the port city of Aden, Yemen. An inset clearly shows a gaping hole in the side of the Arleigh Burke-class destroyer, the result of a blast when a small boat drew alongside the *Cole* and exploded on October 12, 2000. U.S. casualties totaled 17 dead and another 39 wounded.

Terrorism

The Roots of Islamic Terrorism

Most Americans had never heard of al-Qaeda until its infamous attack on their homeland on 9/11. Terrorist attacks were things that occurred elsewhere, in faraway places with funny-sounding names. On September 10, not a single American could have imagined the cataclysmic event about to happen the next day. But happen it did—and Americans entered into a new age of Islamic terror.

Many scholars trace the roots of modern-day Islamic terrorism to Wahhabism. It was founded in 1744 in the Arabian Peninsula by Muhammad ibn Abd al-Wahhab and named for him. He was concerned about the decline of Muslim influence worldwide. He blamed the decline on foreign influences and urged a return to a purer form of Islam that more closely reflected the ideals of the Prophet Muhammad.

Wahhabism is one form of a school of Islam known as Salafiyyah. Early Salifis thought they could reconcile Islamic principles with Western political thought. But later Islamic reformers such as Egyptian writer and activist Sayyid Qutb (1906–66) branded modern Western culture—especially in the United States, where he lived briefly—as barbaric. Qutb called for an ongoing doctrine of jihad to liberate the entire world so that only Islam would prevail. Al-Qaeda answered the call.

Red is the color of blood and this map shows the extent of terrorist attacks across the globe from September 11, 2001 through June 2016.

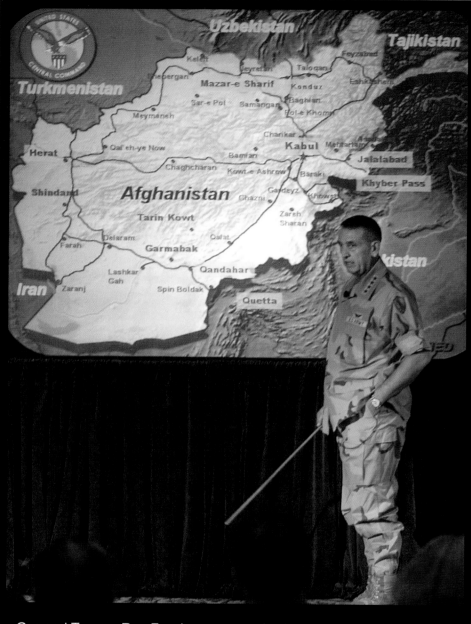

General Tommy Ray Franks, commander-in-chief of the U.S. Central Command (Centcom), stands before a map of Afghanistan while conducting a weekly press briefing in Tampa, Florida, on December 7, 2001. Franks led U.S. forces in the overthrow of the Taliban in Afghanistan in 2001, but failed to capture the elusive Taliban leader Mullah Mohammed Omar or al-Qaeda chief Osama bin Laden. The highly decorated general went on to successfully lead U.S. forces against Saddam Hussein in Iraq in 2003.

CHAPTER 5
By Any Other Name

On the morning of September 11, 2001, President George W. Bush was visiting a second-grade class in Sarasota, Florida. He received news of the attack on the World Trade Center. An hour later, he spoke with Vice President Dick Cheney from high in the sky aboard Air Force One. "We're going to find out who did this and we're going to kick their asses."[1] America's long war on terror had begun.

Three days later, Congress passed an "Authorization for Use of Military Force" against "those nations, organizations or persons [the president] determines planned, authorized, committed or aided the terrorist attacks."[2]

On September 20, Bush addressed both houses of Congress: "Our war on terror begins with al-Qaeda but it does not end there. It will not end until every terrorist group of global reach has been defeated."[3] Such phrasing left the door open for an eventual U.S. incursion into Iraq. The UN Security Council and NATO passed similar measures to combat terrorist acts and respond with force.

After repeated U.S. demands to the Taliban for the release of Osama bin Laden, the Taliban offered to turn him over if the U.S. could supply proof of his guilt. "We know he's guilty. Turn him over,"[4] the president said. The Taliban did not, and the U.S. launched Operation Enduring Freedom. By early December, U.S. and allied forces had seized all of the Taliban-held lands. The Taliban, along with bin Laden and al-Qaeda operatives, dispersed without surrendering. U.S. and United Kingdom forces searched through the caves of Tora Bora—a mountainous area near the Pakistan border—for bin Laden, but he eluded them. The search for him would go on for almost another 10 years.

The action of U.S. forces and their allies toppled the Taliban and denied safe haven to al-Qaeda in Afghanistan, but did not

Wide-eyed and wary, Edress, a 16-year-old anti-Taliban fighter, cautiously explores a cave, partially collapsed by American bombs, in December 2001. The cave—and many like it deep in the Tora Bora mountains of Afghanistan—had been recently occupied by al-Qaeda militants. Osama bin Laden fled through the region's jagged mountains into Pakistan, where he remained hidden for more than nine years.

destroy it. Al-Qaeda soon resurfaced with a bombing attack on the Ghriba synagogue in Tunisia on April 11, 2002. It killed 19 people and wounded more than 30 others. Bombings by al-Qaeda militants continued over the next several years.

In 2003, a wave of bombings in Riyadh targeting living quarters of foreign nationals killed 27, suicide bombings in Casablanca, Morocco killed 33, and an attack on British interests by al-Qaeda affiliates in Turkey claimed the lives of another 27. An attack the following year in Madrid killed 191 people and injured almost 2,000 more. And in 2005, al-Qaeda-inspired British Muslim suicide bombers attacked public transport networks, killing 52 people. Clearly, al-Qaeda was alive and still conducting its odious business.

Casablanca officials examine the devastated exterior of the Hotel Safir, after a suicide bomb attack on May 17, 2003. A series of car bomb attacks in Morocco's largest city killed 33 people and wounded 60 more. Other targets included a Jewish community center, a Spanish cultural center, and the Belgian Consulate. Officials suspected al-Qaeda operatives were responsible.

Terrorists loosely connected to al-Qaeda detonated seven bombs at Madrid's Atocha train station on March 12, 2004. Railway personnel work to remove the wreckage.

Meanwhile, the United States and coalition forces invaded Iraq to oust Iraqi president/dictator Saddam Hussein, seeking to prevent the possible production and use of weapons of mass destruction. In announcing the start of the war to the American public, President Bush cautioned: "These are the opening stages of what will be a broad and concerted effort."[5] The war was fought in two phases: the first phase ended Saddam's regime; the second phase devolved into a long-term struggle in which an **insurgency** emerged to oppose the occupying forces and the newly formed Iraqi government.

This new group was founded and led by Jordanian militant Abu Musab al-Zarqawi. The group pledged allegiance to al-Qaeda and took the name of *Tanzim Qaidat al-Jihad fi Bilad al-Rafi-dayn*—"Al-Qaeda's Organization for Jihad in the Land of the Two Rivers." It soon became better known as Al-Qaeda in Iraq, or AQI.

Al-Zarqawi quickly built a reputation for unrivalled brutality, executing several hostages by knife. He also honed a fine talent for media manipulation, often feeding sensationalist Internet and television outlets with horrendous images of gory executions. Under Zarqawi's leadership, Arab Afghans and other foreign fighters conducted sporadic bombings, kidnappings, and beheadings throughout Iraq.

A photo from the U.S. Department of Defense (DoD) shows al-Qaeda in Iraq (AQI) leader Abu Musab al-Zarqawi amid a cache of automatic weapons. On June 7, 2006, U.S. warplanes bombed a safe house near Baqouba, Iraq, killing al-Zarqawi, his spiritual advisor Sheik Abdul Rahman, and six others.

AQI operated under a four-stage plan. It called for an expansion of the Iraq War by expelling U.S. forces, establishing an Islamic state, exporting the struggle to neighboring secular states, and participating in the Arab-Israeli conflict. Al-Qaeda "core" or "central," as bin Laden's group is often called, continued to spread its brand of terror outside Iraq and around the world.

In 2006, U.S. warplanes caught up with al-Zarqawi north of Baghdad and killed him and several others. Speaking about him from the Rose Garden several hours later, President Bush said, "Through his every action, he sought to defeat America and our coalition partners and turn Iraq into a safe haven from which al-Qaeda could wage its war. . . . Now Zarqawi has met his end, and this violent man will never murder again."[6]

Following Zarqawi's death, Iraqi militias and coalition forces stepped up operations against al-Qaeda in Iraq and weakened its operational capacity. By 2011, the U.S. figured that AQI had been completely destroyed, but it was only briefly defeated. It would live to spread terror another day.

Meanwhile, after nine-plus years of tracking Osama bin Laden, U.S. forces finally caught up with him. In the early morning hours of May 2, 2011, a U.S. Special Forces team of 23 Navy SEALs in Black Hawk helicopters arrived outside a compound in Abbottabad, Pakistan. They breached the outer walls of the compound, fought their way through the first two floors, then up to the third floor where bin Laden lived. Bin Laden fell dead with a gunshot wound to the head, above the left eye. President Barack Obama announced his death to the nation, calling it "the most significant achievement to date in our nation's effort to defeat al-Qaeda."[7]

In December 2011, the United States completed its withdrawal of military forces from Iraq, thereby fulfilling President Barack Obama's campaign promises to end the war in Iraq and bring American troops home. In the months following the U.S. with-

Newspaper headlines herald the death of Osama bin Laden on May 2, 2011. A passerby snaps a photo of the al-Qaeda leader in front of the Newseum in Washington, DC. The night before, U.S. President Barack Obama announced that U.S. Special Forces had killed the most-wanted terrorist in a compound in Abbottabad, Pakistan. After a nine-and-a-half-year pursuit, U.S. forces finally caught up with Osama bin Laden.

drawal, al-Qaeda in Iraq arose from the ashes to continue its quest for a worldwide caliphate. It had a new name (the Islamic State, or IS) and a new leader—Abu Bakr al-Baghdadi. (See *Islamic State* in the Terror, Inc. series.)

In February 2014, following a clash of jihadist ideologies and tactics, current al-Qaeda leader Ayman al-Zawahiri issued a statement online disowning the Islamic State and severing all connections with it. In September, he announced the formation of Al-Qaeda in the Indian Subcontinent (AQIS). Under al-Zawahiri's direction, al-Qaeda continued to grow and expand over the next three years.

At a flag memorial in Lafayette, California, on September 11, 2008, a woman views a montage of images from the 9/11 terrorist attacks on New York City and Washington, DC. Memorials such as this one were held across the country on the seventh anniversary of the 9/11 attacks that killed nearly 3,000 people.

Today, al-Qaeda and its affiliates are alive and active in the Middle East, Africa, Southeast Asia, and elsewhere. Al-Qaeda in the Maghreb (AQIM) operates in North and West Africa. Al-Shabaab ("the Youth") spreads terror in Somalia and East Africa. Al-Qaeda in the Arabian Peninsula (AQAP) controls a vast stretch of land along the southern coast of Yemen. In Syria, Jabhat Fateh al-Sham ("Front for the Conquest of the Levant,"), though a self-proclaimed independent jihadist group, has not publicly disavowed its allegiance to al-Qaeda.

Additionally, according to former Director of National Intelligence James Clapper, al-Qaeda "nodes in Syria, Pakistan, Afghanistan, and Turkey" are "dedicating resources to planning attacks."[8] To date, al-Qaeda has not attempted a major attack on the United States since 2001. But the prospect of another 9/11-sized al-Qaeda event in 2017 or beyond remains ever-present.

Terrorism

Al-Qaeda Today

Countries with significant al-Qaeda activity as of December 2014

United Kingdom · Belgium · Germany · France · Italy · Spain · Syria · Afghanistan · Morocco · Lebanon · Iraq · Algeria · Libya · Pakistan · Mauritania · Saudi Arabia · Yemen · India · Mali · Niger · Kenya · Somalia · Uganda · Tanzania · Philippines · Indonesia

Today's al-Qaeda has come a long way since its inception in Peshawar in the late 1980s. Over the years, it has transformed itself from a tiered organization with a central leadership and a large operating budget into more of a movement of ideas. At first, it trained its own jihadists and sent them afield to carry out attacks. Now, more often than not, it inspires other individuals or allied groups to do its work.

Though its structure and methods may change and evolve, its goals remain the same: to bring about the collapse of the United States and the rest of the Western nations and establish a global caliphate. Ayman al-Zawahiri, al-Qaeda's current chief, hopes to accomplish its aims in three key ways:

first, by accelerating the costs for his adversaries to maintain internal security against the threat of attack;

second, by forcing the expansion of their military presence in the world, along with the cost and commitment of personnel and maintenance;

third, by encouraging powerful foreign competition in trade and commerce (such as from China and India).

With the national debt of the United States standing now near $20 trillion and climbing, Zawahiri's strategy represents a matter of grave concern for all Americans.

TIMELINE

1957 Osama bin Laden is born in Riyadh, Saudi Arabia, on March 10 or July 30.

1978 Leftists overthrow government in Afghanistan in April.

1979 Soviet troops invade Afghanistan to begin the Soviet-Afghan War.

1987 Bin Laden fights heroically against the Soviets at Jaji, Afghanistan in May.

1988 Al-Qaeda founded in Peshawar, Pakistan; bin Laden is named emir.

1989 Soviets pull out of Afghanistan in February; bin Laden returns to Saudi Arabia.

1990 Al-Qaeda operatives lay groundwork for moving headquarters to Sudan; Saddam Hussein's Iraqi Army invades Kuwait on August 2.

1992 *Summer* Al-Qaeda establishes itself in Sudan.

December United States lands troops in Somalia.

December 28 Al-Qaeda operatives set off a bomb at a hotel in Aden, Yemen.

1993 *Early in year* Bin Laden sends a team of military advisors to Somalia.

February 28 Muslim terrorists detonate a van filled with high explosives in the basement of the North Tower of the World Trade Center.

October 3–4 Eighteen American soldiers are killed while trying to capture high-ranking Somalis.

1994 Saudi government strips bin Laden of his citizenship and freezes his remaining assets at home.

1996 Sudan expels bin Laden and he moves to Afghanistan; he issues a fatwa against the United States on August 23.

1997 Bin Laden orders the militarization of al-Qaeda's East African cell.

1998 *February 28* Bin Laden issues a second fatwa against Americans.

August 7 Simultaneous strikes by al-Qaeda at U.S. embassies in Kenya and Tanzania kill 223 people.

August 20 President Bill Clinton orders cruise-missile strikes on al-Qaeda.

2000 Al-Qaeda attack on the guided-missile destroyer USS *Cole* kills 17 American sailors and injures 39.

2001 *September 11* Al-Qaeda terrorists hijack airplanes and fly them into the World Trade Center and the Pentagon; an attempt to fly an airplane into the White House or Capitol building fails.

September 14 Congress passes an "Authorization for Use of Military Force."

September 20 President George W. Bush condemns al-Qaeda in an address to Congress and promises to defeat all terrorist groups with a global reach.

October 4 British Prime Minister Tony Blair reveals Western intelligence information linking Osama bin Laden to Afghanistan's Taliban leadership.

October 7 United States begins bombing Afghanistan.

2002 Al-Qaeda bombs the Ghriba synagogue in Tunisia on April 11.

2003 Bombings in Riyadh, Casablanca, and Turkey kill nearly 100 people.

2004 An attack in Madrid kills 191 people and injures almost 2,000 more; bin Laden admits ordering the 9/11 attacks; al-Qaeda in Iraq, or AQI, is formed.

2005 Al-Qaeda-inspired British Muslim suicide bombers attack public transport networks, killing 52 people.

2006 Abu Musab al-Zarqawi is killed in an airstrike.

2011 Osama bin Laden is killed by U.S. Navy SEALs on May 11.

2012 Al-Qaeda affiliate Ansar al-Sharia in Libya attacks U.S. consulate in Benghazi.

2013 Al-Qaeda in the Maghreb (AQIM) seizes control of a natural gas plant in eastern Algeria.

2014 Two al-Qaeda gunman botch attempt to kidnap U.S. embassy staff in Saana, Yemen.

2015 Abrahim al-Asiri, master bomb-maker with al-Qaeda in the Arabian Peninsula (AQAP), urges lone-wolf-style attacks against America and the West.

2016 Al-Qaeda's online magazine urges would-be jihadists to target American businesses and entrepreneurs to undermine U.S. economy.

2017 U.S. Navy SEAL Petty Officer William "Ryan" Owens is killed in raid on al-Qaeda base in Yemen, along with 14 al-Qaeda members and some 30 civilians.

CHAPTER NOTES

Chapter 1   Two to Remember

1. Philip Sherwell, "9/11: Voices from the doomed planes." *The Telegraph*, London, UK 4:22 PM BST 10 Sep 2011. http://www.telegraph.co.uk/news/worldnews/september-11-attacks/8754395/911-Voices-from-the-doomed-planes.html

2. Ibid.

3. 9/11 Commission. *9/11 Commission Report* (New York: Barnes & Noble, 2006), p. 9.

4. Ibid., p. 11.

5. Ibid.

6. Ibid., p. 13.

7. Sherwell, "9/11."

8. 9/11 Commission, p. 14.

9. Ibid.

10. Ibid.

11. Ibid.

12. START, "Background Report: 9/11, Ten Years Later." http://www.start.umd.edu/sites/default/files/files/announcements/BackgroundReport_10YearsSince9_11.pdf

13. Bret Baier, Ian McCaleb, and Anna Persky of FOX News, and The Associated Press. "Bin Laden Claims Responsibility for 9/11." FoxNews.com. October 30, 2004. http://www.foxnews.com/story/2004/10/30/bin-laden-claims-responsibility-for-11.html

Chapter 2   A New War

1. Peter L. Bergen, *Holy War, Inc.: Inside the Secret World of Osama bin Laden* (New York: The Free Press, 2001), p. 31.

2. Global Research, "Full text of September 2001 Pakistani paper's 'exclusive' interview with Usamah Bin-Laden." http://www.globalresearch.ca/interview-with-osama-bin-laden-denies-his-involvement-in-9-11/24697

3. Yossef Bodansky, *Bin Laden: The Man Who Declared War on America* (Roseville, CA: Forum, 2001), p. 10.

4. Peter L. Bergen, *The Longest War: The Enduring Conflict between America and al-Qaeda* (New York: Free Press, 2011), p. 16.

5. Bergen, *Holy War*, p. 58.

6. John Miller and Michael Stone, with Chris Mitchell, *The Cell: Inside the 9/11 Plot, and Why the FBI and the CIA Failed to Stop It* (New York: Hyperion, 2003), p. 156.

7. Bergen, *Longest War*, p. 17.

8. Ibid., p. 33.

Chapter 3   Building "the Base"

1. Tayseer Allouni, with Usamah bin Laden. "Transcript of Bin Laden's October interview." CNN.com, February 5, 2002. http://edition.cnn.com/2002/WORLD/asiapcf/south/02/05/binladen.transcript/

2. Peter L. Bergen, *The Longest War: The Enduring Conflict between America and al-Qaeda* (New York: Free Press, 2011), p. 18.

3. Ibid., p. 19.

4. Abdel Bari Atwan, *The Secret History of al Qaeda* (Berkeley, CA: University of California Press, 2006), p. 162.

5. Ibid., pp. 221-22.

6. Yossef Bodansky, *Bin Laden: The Man Who Declared War on America* (Roseville, CA: Forum, 2001), pp. 31-32.

Chapter 4   Going Global

1. John Miller and Michael Stone, with Chris Mitchell, *The Cell: Inside the 9/11 Plot, and Why the FBI and the CIA Failed to Stop It* (New York: Hyperion, 2003), pp. 100-01.

2. Ibid., p. 162.

3. Peter L. Bergen, *Holy War, Inc.: Inside the Secret World of Osama bin Laden* (New York: The Free Press, 2001), p. 22.

4. The Heritage Foundation. "Al-Qaeda: Declarations & Acts of War." http://www2.heritage.org/research/projects/enemy-detention/al-qaeda-declarations

5. Ibid.

6. Bergen, *Holy War*, p. 119.

Chapter 5   By Any Other Name

1. Peter L. Bergen, *The Longest War: The Enduring Conflict between America and al-Qaeda* (New York: Free Press, 2011), p. 51.

2. Ibid., p. 59.

3. Ibid., p. 57.

4. Kathy Gannon and Amir Shah, "U.S. Jets Pound Targets Around Kabul." Associated Press, October 15, 2001. http://www.seacoastonline.com/article/20011015/NEWS/310159983

5. Ron Suskind, *The One Percent Doctrine: Deep Inside America's Pursuit of Its Enemies Since 9/11* (New York: Simon & Schuster, 2006), p. 211.

6. Ellen Knickmeyer and Jonathan Finer, "Insurgent Leader Al-Zarqawi Killed in Iraq." *Washington Post*, June 8, 2006. http://www.washingtonpost.com/wp-dyn/content/article/2006/06/08/AR2006060800114.html

7. CNN Library, "Death of Osama Bin Laden Fast Facts." CNN.com, September 9, 2013. http://www.cnn.com/2013/09/09/world/death-of-osama-bin-laden-fast-facts/

8. Thomas Joscelyn, "Fifteen years after the 9/11 attacks, al Qaeda fights on." *Long War Journal*, September 11, 2016. http://www.longwarjournal.com/archives/2016/09/fifteen-years-after-the-911-attacks-al-qaeda-fights-on.php

PRINCIPAL PEOPLE

Peter Arnett—Author and CNN journalist.

Abdullah Azzam (ahb-DUH-lah ah-ZAM)—Radical Palestinian Sunni Islamic scholar and theologian; mentor to Osama bin Laden; founder of Maktab al-Khidamat, or Services Office, in Peshawar, Pakistan.

Abu Bakr al-Baghdadi (AH-boo BAH-kar al-bag-DAH-di)—Leader of the Islamic State.

Abu Ubaidah al-Banshiri (AH-boo oo-BYE-duh al-bahn-SHEER-ee)—Head of al-Qaeda's African presence and second in command of the entire organization.

Omar al-Bashir (OH-mahr al-bah-SHEER)—President of Sudan (1989 to present).

Peter L. Bergen—Author and CNN journalist.

Tony Blair—Prime Minister of the United Kingdom from 1997 to 2007.

George W. Bush—Forty-third President of the United States.

Dick Cheney—Former Vice President of the United States.

Essam Deraz (ESS-em DEHR-az)—an Egyptian filmmaker who covered the battles in Jaji in the spring of 1987.

Jamal al-Fadl (ja-MAHL al-FAHD-uhl)—Sudanese militant member of al-Qaeda and later defector and U.S. informant of al-Qaeda activities.

Turki al-Faisal (TOOR-key al-FIGH-sahl)—Saudi intelligence chief.

Saddam Hussein (sah-DAHM hoo-SAIN)—President and dictator of Iraq (1979-2003).

Faraj Ismail (fah-RAHJ HIS-may-el)—Egyptian journalist who covered the Soviet-Afghan War.

Osama bin Laden (o-SAH-mah bin-LAH-duhn)—Saudi-born leader of al-Qaeda from 1988 to 2011.

Barack Obama—Forty-fourth President of the United States.

Sayyid Qutb (SIGH-yid KUH-tahb)—Egyptian writer and activist.

Mamdouh Mahmoud Salim (MAHM-DOO mah-MOOD SAH-lihm)—Top al-Qaeda official and aide to Osama bin Laden.

Hassan al-Turabi (HAH-sahn al-too-RAH-bee)—Religious and Islamist political leader in Sudan.

Muhammad ibn Abd al-Wahhab (moo-HAH-muhd ib-uhn ab-dahl-wa HAHB)—Founder of Wahhabism in the Arabian Peninsula in 1744.

Abu Musab al-Zarqawi (AH-boo MOO-sahb al zahr-KAW-wee)—Jordanian militant; leader of Al-Qaeda in Iraq (AQI).

Ayman al-Zawahiri (EYE-mahn al-zah-WAH-ree)—Egyptian surgeon and present commander of al-Qaeda.

GLOSSARY

anti-Semitism (AN-tie SEHM-uh-tizm)—opposition or hatred toward the Jewish religion

attrition (uh-TRIH-shun)—gradual lessening of power or strength

coerce (coe-ERSS)—obtain something by using force or the threat of force

emir (ee-MEER)—Muslim leader or ruler

imam (ih-MAHM)—anointed leader; a Muslim spiritual leader

Islam (IS-lahm, or is-LAHM)—the Muslim religion, based on the teachings of the Prophet Muhammad; the Muslim world

fundamentalist (fun-duh-MEHN-tuh-list)—person who believes in a literal, strict interpretation of a religious work

insurgency (in-SUHR-jen-see)—revolt against a government

jihad (ji-HADH)—a holy war undertaken as a sacred duty by Muslims

martyrdom (MAHR-tir-dohm)—the act of undergoing death or great suffering in support of a belief or cause or principle

mujahideen (moo-jah-he-DEEN)—holy warrior; people engaged in jihad, especially in the Middle East; also spelled mujahedeen and mujahedin

nominal (NAHM-uh-nuhl)—in name only

primeval (pry-MEE-vuhl)—the earliest ages in world history

profane (proh-FANE)—disrespectful of religious practice

Quran (kuh-RAN)—book composed of sacred writings accepted by Muslims as revelations made to Muhammad by Allah through the angel Gabriel

Pentagon (PEN-tuh-gahn)—Five-sided building in Washington D.C. that is the headquarters of the U.S. Defense Department

psyche (SIGH-kee)—soul or mind of an individual or group

secular (SEK-yew-lahr)—concerned with worldly affairs rather than spiritual ones; an opposition to or rejection of religion

solicitor general (so-LIH-suh-tohr GEN-ehr-uhl)—third-ranking position in the U.S. Department of Justice; person who represents the federal government before the Supreme Court

Sunnah (SUN-nuh)—practices, customs, and traditions of the Prophet Muhammad; body of work that constitutes the proper observance of Islam

ulema (oo-LEM-ah)—body of Islamic scholars

umma (UM-mah)—Islamic nation or community of believers

unindicted co-conspirators (un-in-DIE-tuhd coh-cuhn-SPIHR-uh-torz)—persons engaged in a conspiracy but not charged with a particular crime

wax lyrically (WAKS LEER-uh-cuh-lee)—speak or write enthusiastically

FURTHER READING

Green, Robert. *Cause & Effect: The September 11 Attacks*. Cause & Effect in History Series. San Diego, CA: Reference Point Press, 2015.

Landau, Elaine. *Osama bin Laden: The Life and Death of the 9/11 al-Qaeda Mastermind*. Minneapolis, MN: Twenty-First Century Books (Lerner), 2011.

————. *Suicide Bombers: Foot Soldiers of the Terrorist Movement*. Minneapolis, MN: Twenty-First Century Books (Lerner), 2006.

Miller, Mara. *Remembering September 11, 2001*. What We Know Now Series. Berkeley Heights, NJ: Enslow Publishers, 2011.

Williams, Julie. *Islam: Understanding the History, Beliefs, and Culture*. Issues in Focus Today Series. Berkeley Heights, NJ: Enslow Publishers, 2008.

WORKS CONSULTED

Allouni, Tayseer, with Usamah bin Laden. "Transcript of Bin Laden's October interview." CNN.com, February 5, 2002. http://edition.cnn.com/2002/WORLD/asiapcf/south/02/05/binladen.transcript/

Atwan, Abdel Bari. *The Secret History of al Qaeda*. Berkeley, CA: University of California Press, 2006.

Baier, Bret, Ian McCaleb, and Anna Persky of FOX News, and The Associated Press. "Bin Laden Claims Responsibility for 9/11." FoxNews.com. October 30, 2004. http://www.foxnews.com/story/2004/10/30/bin-laden-claims-responsibility-for-11.html

Bergen, Peter L. *The Longest War: The Enduring Conflict between America and al-Qaeda*. New York: Free Press, 2011.

————. *Holy War, Inc.: Inside the Secret World of Osama bin Laden*. New York: Free Press, 2001.

Burke, Jason. *Al-Qaeda: The True Story of Radical Islam*. 3d ed. New York: Penguin Books, 2007.

Carr, Caleb. *The Lessons of Terror: A History of Warfare against Civilians: Why It Has Always Failed and Why It Will Fail Again*. New York: Random House, 2002.

CNN Library. "Death of Osama Bin Laden Fast Facts." CNN.com, September 9, 2013. http://www.cnn.com/2013/09/09/world/death-of-osama-bin-laden-fast-facts/

Coll, Steve. *Ghost Wars: The Secret History of the CIA, Afghanistan, and bin Laden, from the Soviet Invasion to September 10, 2001*. New York: Penguin Press, 2004.

Gannon, Kathy, and Amir Shah. "U.S. Jets Pound Targets Around Kabul." Associated Press, October 15, 2001. http://www.seacoastonline.com/article/20011015/NEWS/310159983

WORKS CONSULTED

Global Research. "Full text of September 2001 Pakistani paper's 'exclusive' interview with Usamah Bin-Laden." http://www.globalresearch.ca/interview-with-osama-bin-laden-denies-his-involvement-in-9-11/24697

Joscelyn, Thomas. "Fifteen years after the 9/11 attacks, al Qaeda fights on." *Long War Journal,* September 11, 2016. http://www.longwarjournal.com/archives/2016/09/fifteen-years-after-the-911-attacks-al-qaeda-fights-on.php

Knickmeyer, Ellen, and Jonathan Finer, "Insurgent Leader Al-Zarqawi Killed in Iraq." *Washington Post,* June 8, 2006. http://www.washingtonpost.com/wp-dyn/content/article/2006/06/08/AR2006060800114.html

9/11 Commission. *9/11 Commission Report.* New York: Barnes & Noble, 2006.

Sela, Avraham. *The Continuum Political Encyclopedia of the Middle East.* Revised and updated ed. New York: Continuum, 2002.

Sherwell, Philip. "9/11: Voices from the doomed planes." *The Telegraph,* London, UK 4:22PM BST 10 Sep 2011. http://www.telegraph.co.uk/news/worldnews/september-11-attacks/8754395/911-Voices-from-the-doomed-planes.html

START. "Background Report: 9/11, Ten Years Later." http://www.start.umd.edu/sites/default/files/files/announcements/BackgroundReport_10YearsSince9_11.pdf

Suskind, Ron. *The One Percent Doctrine: Deep Inside America's Pursuit of Its Enemies Since 9/11.* New York: Simon & Schuster, 2006

Yossef, Bodansky. *Bin Laden: The Man Who Declared War on America.* Roseville, CA: Forum, 2001.

ON THE INTERNET

Gaynor, Tim, and Tiemoko Diallo. "Al Qaeda linked to rogue aviation network." http://www.reuters.com/assets/print?aid=USTRE60C3E820100113

Hayes, Laura, Borgna Brunner, and Beth Rowen. "Al-Qaeda: Osama bin Laden's Network of Terror." http://www.infoplease.com/spot/al-qaeda-terrorism.html

Reichman, Deb, Associated Press. "How strong is al-Qaida today?" http://www.pbs.org/newshour/rundown/strong-al-qaida-today/

INDEX